VOICES OF THE ALAMO

VOICES OF

WRITTEN BY SHERRY GARLAND

THE ALAMO

ILLUSTRATED BY RONALD HIMLER

SCHOLASTIC PRESS ◆ NEW YORK

ACKNOWLEDGMENTS:
Special thanks to Dr. Richard Bruce Winders, Historian and Curator, the Alamo,
who reviewed the manuscript and art for historical accuracy, and to Julia Mercedes Castilla
and Teresa Mlawer for their help with the Spanish words.

Library of Congress Cataloging-in-Publication Data
Garland, Sherry.
Voices of the Alamo / by Sherry Garland; illustrated by Ronald Himler. – 1st ed.   p. cm.
Includes bibliographical references.
Summary: From the 1500s to the present, different voices and perspectives of men and women—Indian, Mexican, Spanish, Texian,
and American—recount the history of the Alamo and its region.
ISBN 0-590-98833-6
1. Alamo (San Antonio, Tex.)—History Juvenile literature. 2. Alamo (San Antonio, Tex.) Biography Juvenile literature. 3. Alamo
(San Antonio, Tex.)—Siege, 1836 Juvenile literature. 4. Texas—History—To 1846 Juvenile literature. [1. Alamo (San Antonio,
Tex.)—Siege, 1836. 2. Alamo (San Antonio, Tex.)—History. 3. Texas—History—Revolution, 1835–1836.] I. Himler, Ronald, ill.
II. Title. F390.G23   2000   976.4'351—dc21   99-18274   CIP

10 9 8 7 6 5 4 3 2 1   0/0 01 02 03 04

Printed in Hong Kong   38
First edition, March 2000
Book design by David Caplan
The text type was set in 15-point Treusdell.
The display type was set in 92-point Sanvito 364 Regular.
The illustrations in this book were rendered in watercolor and gouache.

To Mrs. Mary Galvan, my high school English teacher,

who taught me the beauty and power of language;

who ignited my desire to be a writer;

and who encouraged me to enter a writing contest

with an essay that began, "I've never seen the Alamo." — S. G.

1500

I am a Payaya maiden,
gathering pecans beside the river.
When flowers blanket these hills in spring
and buffalo thunder across the plains,
my heart sings with joy.
But this earth does not belong to me,
for who can own the wind or rain?

1542

I am a bold *conquistador*,
born and raised in Spain.
Upon my swift and mighty steed, with sword in hand,
I search for cities of gold and take what I please.
I christen this place great land of the Tejas,
and claim all that lies before me
in the name of God and of the king.

1745

We are humble padres
with bare feet and robes of gray,
come to save the souls of the gentle natives here.
Beside this peaceful river called San Antonio,
we built a mission of chalky white stones
cut from the hills nearby.
The walls are thick and strong enough to last forever,
but I fear this land is too wild to be tamed.

1803

I am a Spanish soldier,
biding time in this abandoned mission
whose unfinished roof lets in
winter snows and summer rains.
We call this fort the "Alamo,"
the word for cottonwood tree.
We planted cannons
where crosses used to stand;
we polish our swords in dusty cells
where padres used to pray,
and keep our eyes open
for enemies of the king
under a moonlit sky.

1821

I am a Tejano rancher,
born and raised in Texas
like my father before me.
The guitars will sing at the *hacienda* tonight,
for the rule of the Spanish king across the sea has ended,
and Mexico is free at last.
¡Viva la libertad! ¡Viva México!

1830

I am a Texian farmer
who followed Stephen Austin
from the United States to this wilderness
where few Mexicans choose to live.
I cleared the woods and tilled the soil;
I fought off endless Indian raids
and watched my children die from fevers.
It is a harsh life we lead, but this land is mine,
and I will love Texas forever.

1834

I am Antonio López de Santa Anna,
general of all the Mexican army
and beloved El Presidente since 1833.
These ungrateful Texians annoy me greatly.
They swore to be loyal citizens of Mexico,
but still they cling to their American ways
and complain about all I do.
New scoundrels come in droves, illegally taking Mexican lands,
until now there are tenfold more English-speaking Texians
than loyal Spanish-speaking Mexicans.
I shall raise their taxes and take away their rights;
I shall abolish the precious Constitution of 1824
that those Texians admire so well;
I shall drive those disgruntled ruffians
back from where they came.

1835

I am Sarah Seely DeWitt
from the town of Gonzales.
When Mexican dragoons demanded our little cannon —
a useless ol' thing that wouldn't hurt a fly —
I tore up my daughter's wedding gown
to sew a flag for our boys and men.
Come and Take It! we stitched in big, bold letters,
and I'm proud to say our flag waved victoriously
as our boys in buckskins chased those soldiers away,
then marched on to San Antonio
and later seized that old mission called the Alamo.
One thing deeply worries me, though —
that humiliated Mexican general they defeated there
was Santa Anna's own brother-in-law.

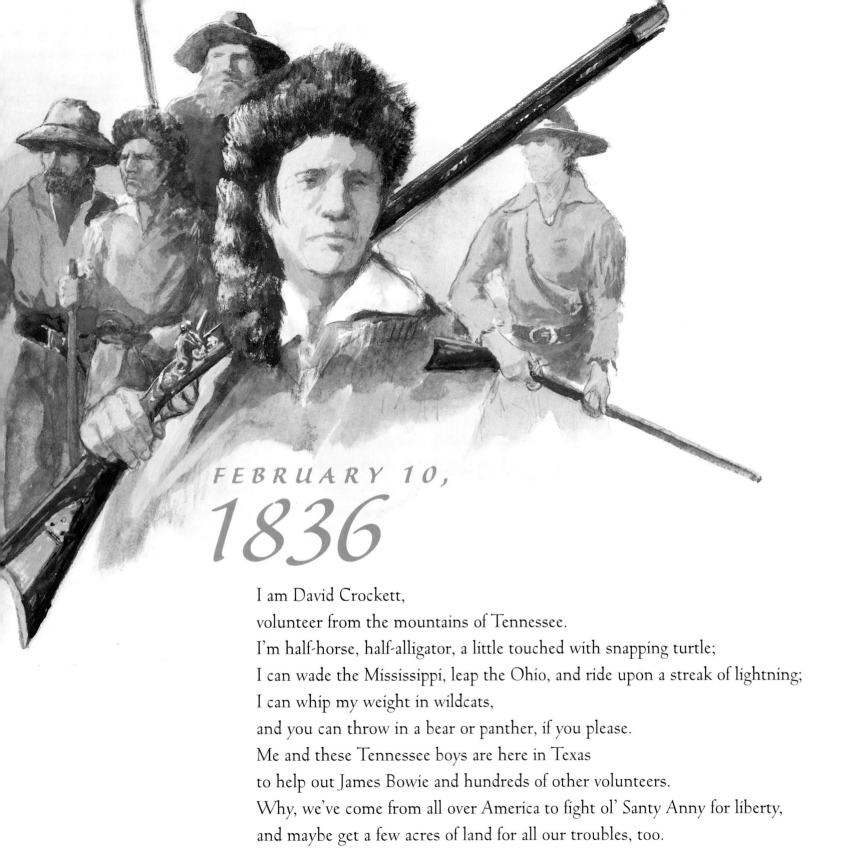

FEBRUARY 10,

1836

I am David Crockett,

volunteer from the mountains of Tennessee.

I'm half-horse, half-alligator, a little touched with snapping turtle;

I can wade the Mississippi, leap the Ohio, and ride upon a streak of lightning;

I can whip my weight in wildcats,

and you can throw in a bear or panther, if you please.

Me and these Tennessee boys are here in Texas

to help out James Bowie and hundreds of other volunteers.

Why, we've come from all over America to fight ol' Santy Anny for liberty,

and maybe get a few acres of land for all our troubles, too.

FEBRUARY 23,
1836

I am a poor peasant
from the valleys of Mexico.
One day soldiers dragged me from my cornfield
and forced me to join El Presidente's army,
to fight in his latest war.
Death haunted us for hundreds of leagues
as four thousand men and mules
marched over the rugged mountains and deserts,
through the bitter blizzards,
with little food or water or blankets
to protect our bare feet from the snow.
When I arrived today at the river called San Antonio,
my sergeant shoved a musket into my hands
and pointed me at an old mission
whose chalky white walls glisten in the winter sun.

MARCH 5,
1836

I am William Barret Travis,
commander of the Alamo.
When that arrogant general,
with his silver saddle and golden sword,
called for our surrender, I answered with a cannon shot
and told him it would be victory or death for us.
His blood-red flag flying from the church steeple
reminds us daily there will be no quarter in the final fight.
For twelve days we have held back the siege,
and more Mexican soldiers arrive each day.
I have sent letters pleading for help from everyone I know,
but now there is no hope; our fate is sealed.
Tonight I scratched a line in the sand with my sword and said,
"Cross this line if you will stand and fight with me,
but know that surely you will die."
All but one of the volunteers stepped forward,
and now we wait for our destiny to be fulfilled.

MARCH 6,
1836
BEFORE DAWN

I am a drummer
in Santa Anna's army,
following a column of wary men.
Just past midnight, while the night wind whispered
through the trees and over the mission walls,
the soldiers said their prayers
and fixed their bayonets,
then crossed the peaceful river in silence.
Lying on the cold, cold ground,
we look at the Alamo now,
so quiet and still and near.
We wait.
And shiver.
And wait.

MARCH 6, 1836

I am Susanna Dickinson, wife of Almeron.
Early this morning, before the sun streaked the sky,
I heard Mexican trumpets shriek a blood-chilling sound,
and as drummers thumped out a steady beat,
four shouting columns of soldiers charged these shadowy mission walls.
The roar of cannonade and the crack of Kentucky rifles
and the shouts of dying men filled the cold, smoky air.
In the chapel where we women and our children huddled and trembled with fear,
my beloved husband kissed our baby girl good-bye forever.
Not long after that, the cannons stood silent — and it was over.

APRIL 21,
1836

I am General Sam Houston,
and luck was with my ragged Texas army today.
In these boggy bayous of the San Jacinto River,
six weeks after that futile bloodshed at the Alamo,
and the unforgivable massacre at Goliad,
we caught El Presidente off guard, taking a siesta in his silken tent.
As my men chased the fleeing foe, they screamed out in a frenzy,
"Remember Goliad! Remember the Alamo!"
Independence is ours, and now Texas is a republic
with a government of its own.

1904

I am Miss Clara Driscoll,
and it saddens my heart to see
this precious old mission crumbling
and ignored for so many years.
Buildings have sprouted up all around,
squeezing the Alamo chapel out of sight.
Since Texas joined the Union in 1845
and became the Lone Star State,
the mission has been a U. S. army depot,
a Confederate armory, and a general store
and warehouse filled with dry goods and beans.
Chili vendors and merchants peddle their wares
from the backs of wagons on the plaza.
Now, sir, you tell me you want to tear down
these sacred barracks to build another hotel?
Does no one care what happened here
that cold spring morning so long ago?
Miss Adina De Zavala and the Daughters of the Republic
are collecting money to purchase these hallowed barrack walls,
and if their funds fall short, I will buy the building myself,
for we must never forget the lesson of the Alamo.

Today

I saw the Alamo
for the first time today.
We tourists shuffled through the heavy doors
to stare at Bowie knives and faded letters under glass.
Later, as I listened to the sound of rustling live oak leaves
and the gentle crackle of the Texas flag,
I thought I heard a voice say,
"Who will remember me?"

Who the voice belonged to, I cannot say,
maybe Texian, maybe Mexican,
maybe Spanish padre, maybe Indian child,
but surely it was some lonesome soul
who lost his life so long ago.
The words echoed over the barracks,
and over the chalky white mission walls,
over the blackened cannons now silent and cold,
over the city streets and souvenir shops
and glass shopping malls,
and over the rolling hills.

"Who will remember me?"
the voice sighed again.

"We will," I whispered to the wind.
"We will remember you."

For thousands of years before the Battle of the Alamo, Native Americans inhabited the area that is now called Texas. Several hunting-and-gathering groups, including the Payaya, lived in the region near San Antonio.

Spaniards first came to Texas in 1519. In 1542, in search of gold, the Spanish *conquistador* Coronado led an expedition to the area and encountered the Teyas (or Tejas) Indians. Although some scholars believe Texas got its name from those Indians, others feel it came from the Caddo Indian word *tayshas*, which means "friend."

In the late 1600s, to thwart French encroachment into Texas, Spain authorized the establishment of missions and *presidios*. In 1718, Franciscan padres built Mission San Antonio de Valero and began converting local Indians to Catholicism. Over the years, this mission faced many problems: The native population shrank due to diseases unwittingly introduced by the Spaniards; it was persistently attacked by Apache and Comanche Indians; and the bell tower and roof of the chapel fell in. In the late 1700s, the Church closed the mission.

In 1803, because of new concerns about foreign encroachment, Spanish cavalry soldiers were sent to the mission. This "Second Flying Company of San Carlos de Alamo de Parras," also referred to as the "Alamo Company," used the mission as a fort and gave it its common name — the Alamo.

Mexico, a Spanish colony, declared its independence from Spain in 1821 after an eleven-year struggle. The Alamo soldiers came under the rule of the Mexican army and Texas became part of a state called "Coahuila y Texas" in the Republic of Mexico. Mexicans living in Texas were called Tejanos. Cattle ranching was one of their main occupations.

The new Mexican government encouraged foreigners to come to Texas. *Empresarios* such as Stephen Austin and Green DeWitt made contracts with the Mexican government to bring in hundreds of American settlers. The land grants were generous and the terms appealing, with no taxes for several years. The settlers, mostly Protestant Anglos who called themselves Texians, agreed to convert to Catholicism and pledge allegiance to the Mexican Constitution of 1824, which had been partially modeled after the American constitution. North Americans flooded to the region, thousands of them illegally, and by 1835 there were almost ten times as many English-speaking Texians as Spanish-speaking Tejanos.

Always seething with internal problems, the Republic of Mexico began changing its laws regarding Texas and prohibited the immigration of North Americans. The Mexican president elected in 1833, General Antonio López de Santa Anna, a war hero and self-proclaimed dictator, replaced the Mexican Constitution of 1824. Taxes were levied and Mexican convicts were sent to live and work in Texas. Further, most Texians did not assimilate into Mexican culture, refusing to learn Spanish or convert to Catholicism. Unrest grew among the Texians as well as among some Tejanos. Talk of war and independence from Mexico spread.

Matters came to a head when Mexico sent soldiers to a Texian settlement, Gonzales, to confiscate an old cannon that had been used against the Comanche. The colonists filled the cannon with nails and scrap iron and waved a homemade flag that defiantly proclaimed *Come and Take It!* Although many Texians wanted to remain loyal Mexican citizens and restore the 1824 constitution, that cannon shot of October 2, 1835, officially launched the Texas revolution. The rough-clad Texians won that battle, and marched on to fight Mexican troops garrisoned at the Alamo in San Antonio de Béxar. In December 1835, an army of Texians, Tejanos, and American volunteers won the Battle of Béxar, seizing the Alamo. They released the captured Mexican soldiers and their general, who was Santa Anna's brother-in-law.

Word of an impending war had already spread throughout the United States, and volunteer companies began organizing. One of the groups that came to Texas was the Tennessee Volunteers, which included the famous frontiersman and former congressman, David Crockett. Another well-known Tennessee man, Sam Houston, was put in command of the new Texas Army. Houston advised that the Alamo be destroyed, but the Alamo leaders decided to stay and defend it.

Infuriated at his brother-in-law's humiliating defeat and determined to drive what he considered "traitors" from Mexican lands, General Santa Anna quickly organized for the Texas campaign. Four thousand soldiers set out from central Mexico on an excruciating forced march in the dead of winter. Many of the soldiers were untrained peasants and Indians conscripted into service. Through blizzards and over treacherous desert terrain, with little food, water, or warm clothing, hundreds died along the way. Santa Anna and the 1,000-man vanguard arrived at San Antonio de Béxar on February 23, 1836. They hoisted a blood-red flag signaling "no quarter" — no man inside the Alamo would be spared.

Approximately 200 men — Texian colonists, American volunteers, and Tejanos — took refuge inside the old mission-fort. The thirteen-day Siege of the Alamo began. After James Bowie, a famous knife-fighting adventurer, became fatally ill, command of the Alamo fell upon the shoulders of a young Texian lawyer, William Barret Travis. In a series of messages, Travis pleaded for reinforcements. Only thirty-two men from Gonzales came to his aid. According to one account, seeing all was hopeless, Travis drew a line in the sand with his sword and gave his men the choice to stay and surely die or to leave.

More Mexican troops continued to arrive. On March 5, Santa Anna set into play a major assault. His soldiers awoke at midnight and prepared their gear. Divided into four columns, they crossed the river under the cover of darkness and by four A.M. were in position near the Alamo.

In the cold, pre-dawn hours of Sunday, March 6, 1836, Santa Anna's columns charged the fort as trumpeters played an ominous tune. The battle raged furiously. The north Alamo wall was eventually breached and intense hand-to-hand combat followed. Mexican casualties were heavy, but in the end, all of the defenders were killed. A few women and children, one male Tejano, and one male slave were spared. The only Anglo survivors were Susanna Dickinson and her young daughter, Angelina.

Upon learning of the fall of the Alamo, thousands of colonists fled eastward in what became known as the "Runaway Scrape." The Mexican army followed not far behind. Drenched by heavy rains, forced to cross swollen rivers, and afflicted with diseases, hundreds of civilians died. Further south, in the town of Goliad, 400 captured, unarmed Texas Volunteers were killed by order of Santa Anna. News of the massacre inflamed the Texian populace. General Houston and his retreating army waited for the right moment to strike. On April 21, seeing that the Mexican army had been divided into three parts, Houston attacked Santa Anna's forces near the San Jacinto River during their afternoon siesta. The Rebels defeated the startled Mexican forces. Santa Anna, who tried to escape disguised as a private, was captured and forced to order the withdrawal of all Mexican troops from Texas. He later signed a treaty recognizing Texas as an independent republic. The Mexican government, however, never considered the treaty legitimate.

The Republic of Texas lasted until December 1845, when Texas joined the United States as the twenty-eighth state. Mexico, who still claimed Texas, and the United States immediately went to war. The Mexican War lasted until 1848, when Mexico was defeated and forced to relinquish claim to Texas, California, and today's southwestern states. During that war, the U.S. army finally built a roof for the Alamo chapel, installing the famous "hump," as we know it today.

Over the following years, the Alamo buildings were used for storage and fell into disrepair. In 1883, the State of Texas purchased the chapel, but by 1904, the barracks were in danger of being torn down to make way for a new hotel. Under the leadership of Adina De Zavala, the Daughters of the Republic of Texas collected funds to save the historic structure. When contributions fell short, Clara Driscoll put up $65,000 and bought the barracks herself. She gave the title to the State of Texas and eventually the barracks were restored and made into a museum.

Today the Alamo is maintained by the Daughters of the Republic of Texas. Thousands of visitors come to view the artifacts inside the museum and chapel. The original mission plaza and outer walls have long been torn down and replaced by the hotels and skyscrapers of modern-day San Antonio.

Although most people think of the Battle of the Alamo as a part of Texas and Mexico's history, the events there helped shape the future of the entire United States, too. In fact, the defenders came from at least twenty-two American states and six foreign nations. Only nine were born in Texas — the nine Tejanos of Mexican ancestry. The defenders came to Texas for many reasons. Some were running away from unsavory pasts, while others were there for glory or greed, to defend their farms and families, or to fight against what they perceived as tyranny. Most were young — the average man being twenty-nine years old. William Travis himself was only twenty-six, while David Crockett was considered an old man at age forty-nine. The defenders of the Alamo were ordinary men, yet their bravery against insurmountable odds and their final act of courage earned them a place in the pages of history forever.

◆ G L O S S A R Y ◆

ANGLO (ANG-loe)—an English-speaking person of British ancestry

CONQUISTADOR (khon-kees-tah-DOR)—a Spaniard who conquered the New World, especially in the sixteenth century

EL PRESIDENTE (el preh-see-DEHN-tay)—the president

EMPRESARIO (ehm-preh-SAH-ree-o)—a contractor, specifically a person who contracted with the Mexican government to bring settlers to Texas

HACIENDA (ah-see-EN-dah)—a large ranch or farm

PADRE (PAH-dray)—father; specifically a Catholic priest

PRESIDIO (preh-SEE-dee-o)—a fort, specifically one built near a mission

SIESTA (see-ES-tah)—an afternoon rest period, typically after the midday meal

TAYSHAS (TAY-shash)—the Caddo Indian word for friend

TEJANO (tay-HAHN-o)—someone of Mexican ancestry living in Texas

TEJAS (TAY-hahs)—the original Spanish spelling of Texas

¡VIVA LA LIBERTAD! (VEE-vah lah lee-bayr-TAHD)—Long live freedom!

¡VIVA MÉXICO! (VEE-vah MEH-hee-koe)—Long live Mexico!

SELECTED BIBLIOGRAPHY

CHARITON, WALLACE O. *100 Days in Texas: The Alamo Letters.* Plano, TX: Wordware Publishing, Inc., 1990.

DE LA PEÑA, JOSÉ ENRIQUE. *With Santa Anna in Texas: A Personal Narrative of the Revolution.* College Station, TX: Texas A&M Press, 1975.

HARDIN, STEPHEN L. *Texian Iliad: A Military History of the Texas Revolution.* Austin: University of Texas Press, 1996.

LONG, JEFF. *Duel of Eagles: The Mexican and U.S. Fight for the Alamo.* New York: William Morrow, 1990.

LORD, WALTER. *A Time to Stand: The Epic of the Alamo.* Lincoln, NE: University of Nebraska Press, 1961.

NELSON, GEORGE. *The Alamo: An Illustrated History.* Uvalde, TX: Aldine Press, 1998.

RATHER, ETHEL ZIVLEY. "DeWitt's Colony." *The Quarterly of the Texas State Historical Association,* Vol. VIII, No. 2 (October 1904): 95-192.

SUGGESTIONS FOR FURTHER READING

BREDESEN, CARMEN. *The Battle of the Alamo: The Fight for Texas Territory.* Brookfield, CT: Millbrook Press, 1996.

CARTER, ALDEN R. *Last Stand at the Alamo.* Danbury, CT: Franklin Watts, 1990.

GARLAND, SHERRY. *A Line in the Sand: The Alamo Diary of Lucinda Lawrence.* New York: Scholastic Inc., 1998.

JAKES, JOHN. *Susanna of the Alamo: A True Story.* San Diego: Harcourt Brace Jovanovich, 1986.

SORRELS, ROY. *The Alamo in American History.* Springfield, NJ: Enslow Publishers, 1996.

SULLIVAN, GEORGE. *Alamo!* New York: Scholastic Inc., 1997.